L O V E L Y ,

R A S P B E R R Y

Also by Aaron Belz

The Bird Hoverer

LOVELY,

RASPBERRY

POEMS

AARON BELZ

A KAREN & MICHAEL BRAZILLER BOOK
PERSEA BOOKS/NEW YORK

Thanks to the editors of the following publications in which certain poems
first appeared, sometimes in earlier versions or under different titles: *88,
Another Chicago Magazine, Anti-Poetry, Black Clock, Boston Review, Can We
Have Our Ball Back, Carve, The Canary, Cimarron Review, Court Green, Drunken
Boat, Eleven Eleven, Fence, Fine Madness, Gulf Coast, Jacket, La République
Mondiale des Lettres, Margie, Melancholia's Tremulous Dreadlocks, The New
Pantagruel, No Tell Motel, Painted Bride Quarterly, Pierogi Press, Poems-for-All,
Shampoo, Sitaudis, Van Gogh's Ear, The Washington Post*

Persea Books, Inc.
853 Broadway
New York, NY 10003

Library of Congress Cataloging-in-
Publication Data

Belz, Aaron, 1971-
Lovely, raspberry : poems / Aaron Belz.-- 1st ed.
    p. cm.
"A Karen & Michael Braziller Book."
ISBN 978-0-89255-359-4 (original trade pbk. : alk. paper)
I. Title.
PS3602.E463L68 2010
811'.6--dc22

                    2009051234

Design by Dinah Fried and Joe Marianek

First edition

Printed in the United States of America

contents

direction

You expect me to tell you about the interior of the room
in which I'm typing this, and connect that to my feelings,
but I'd rather tell you about the interior of your room
and use that as a symbol for something less abstract.

Actually, here's a better idea. Let's put our heads together
and try to think up a third room unknown to either of us,
then divide or multiply its number of windows by the least
number of words necessary to describe it.

In this way perhaps we can accurately triangulate
brief but nearly photographic images of each other's
mothers when they were first married, in veils,
and of their driving down the street with tin-can tails,

of their first orgasmic separation, their little giggles,
and of their medication when it came time to prescribe it.
You expect me to tell you about the spite in my loin
which is the sad hail of commas in the professor's paragraph,

but I cannot even begin to do it, for I am a ranch boy
and not even a very good one; I live in El Bandito, Texas.
I am an old man in Maine, I manage a dime store,
and you, you are a movie director, but only in your mind.

critique

That's not very good.
Try doing that differently.
That's not very good either.
You're not very good at this.

the love-hat relationship

I have been thinking about the love-hat relationship.
It is the relationship based on love of one another's hats.
The problem with the love-hat relationship is that it is superficial.
You don't necessarily even know the other person.
Also it is too dependent on whether the other person
is even wearing the favored hat. We all enjoy hats,
but they're not something to build an entire relationship on.
My advice to young people is to like hats but not love them.
Try having like-hat relationships with one another.
See if you can find something interesting about
the personality of the person whose hat you like.

my chiquita

We were friends. We dressed up as bananas
sometimes and went out on the town.
I called her my Chiquita. All in good fun.
We talked about dating—whether we should
make our relationship official. We decided no.
We were happy to have the freedom
of just being friends with banana outfits.

you bore me

You bore me. So be it.
I bore you and enjoy doing it.
Let us learn to bore each other
without worrying about it.
You act all shy around me,

and that's your prerogative.
If I act shy around you,
it's because you're pretty
and I want to kiss you.
I wish I were Canadian.

If I were Canadian,
I could be boring and
get away with it. You'd say,
This man is from Canada.
He bores me. He acts shy.

He wants to kiss me.
And you would let me
kiss you not only on the lips
but on the cheek, neck,
shoulder; belly, maybe?

Because I would be Canadian
and have scruffy hair
and big eyes. But, alas,
you bore me, too. You
act like you're from Michigan.

honeymoon in altai

Or stroke the good, serious face of a horse!
— Solzhenitsyn

At one, we observed a monkey.
At seven, I made lemonade.

At one, I doffed my yellow Kangol.
At seven, we kissed in bed.

At one, we spat in the pool.
At seven, I checked the Weather Channel.

At one, I chopped up cake.
At seven, we ate crab and lettuce.

At one, we froze in our lacies.
At seven, I lay abed.

la vie

It rains, *il pleut,* all over
my grounds. It blows,
le vent, the treetops around.

I love *mon papillon*
as she's waking up
among twisted sheets;

I love *ma belle*
as she grinds beans
for our morning cup.

Cher vent, come sow
your thoughts in the ground.
Bring us *de l'eau,*

coarse trees, fresh streets,
white lies— old hat
under these new skies.

what

Every day I get emails
that say things like
BELZ! We should
have done that one
thing that one
time, remember?
Really though
how ARE things?

And I always reply
the same way,
like, DUDE!
I do not know
who you are.
Where do I know
you from?
But I never hear back.

I save all those emails
in a special folder
labeled "I hate my life."

reinventing the wheel

I tried to reinvent the wheel, and it was fun,
because I did. It came out better than before,
rounder, quicker, and with less friction.
The mistake I made was trying to reinvent you:
you came out taller and less confident,
with a shopkeeper's eye and shiny skin.
You got me back by reinventing me,
turning me into what I had wanted to be,
a pensive, slightly overweight woman
with a knack for arcane geography.
Will we be happy as our new selves?
I ask myself as we lean back with brandies
on a moonlit night; I think we will,
I think to myself, though I'm thinking it as you,
and you're looking down on me as I would,
as if at any minute I might steal something,
but still not knowing what is in my mind—
a peninsula where it rains but never snows.

gifts

I gave you a digital compact hi-fi system,
but it didn't work.

It sounded like a tuba player dying.

You gave me an onyx-encrusted watch
that shone on my wrist.

Our orchestra wheezed at the lake's edge,
waxed Jaguars roaming the roads.

You gave me a kiss, and I gave you one
under stuffed stars and their muted sunshine.

It was a matter of Kinsey versus Pont-du-Lac,
and you had bet on Pont-du-Lac.

It sounded like commentators mumbling.

Our oedipal complexes lay dormant for a night
while solipsistic rock stars mingled,
their V-12 engines waiting, purring.

Our engagement produced more than crystal
tinkling, but not much more.

I gave you three bracelets, one for each song
we had heard, but one broke.

You gave me your gaze, your generosity,
and most of all, your fiery lashing tongue,
you Mona. You Queen of Scots.

It was a matter of Kinsey versus Pont-du-Lac,
and I had bet on Kinsey.

privacy

When every word sounds cliché,
each turn of phrase derivative,
that's when I turn to slapstick
and boorish sexual innuendo.

Usually, in a real beer garden,
tables are heavier, harder to topple,
glasses sit thickly amidst condensation,
and a river goes on and on nearby.

Sometimes thunder wakes
every phosphorescent sea-animal
while its accompanying lightning
photointegrates itself with leaves.

Christy came toward our party
without elegance, stumbling in her boots,
a can of Carlsberg in each hand,
and I was on my cell phone.

"They wanted the hemmed garments
that lay nestled among antiques
lifted up and glorified in the sun
and left out to bake the mold away.

"They winced at porticoes that sat
as if emancipated from roofs,
because they glared so wholesomely
and because they were so beautiful."

Encapsulated thus, her thoughts
became as fine night smokes
that curl together up under
their table's striped umbrella,

and without even needing to embarrass
myself I stood up and excused myself,
crisscrossed the gravelly center garden
as a drop, and then another drop, fell.

ginkgoes

It was a weird weekend weatherwise.
Stuff touched down, from funnels to hail kernels,
all along the sickle-like coast of Vladivostok,
where we were renting a room full of beds
and windows—awful little windows with
white wire security screens stapled to them,
keeping out everything but the June bugs and flies.

Vladivostok *et ses environs*, which included
the Gulf of Love, as it was known in those days,
had suffered the severest famine in seventy years
under the untrained oversight of Lustful Leonid,
a social smoker with a few extra pounds,
a controversial appointment of the former Tsarina.
Well, at least our *hostellerie* was secluded.

I thought of you when I explored the creek banks,
a place overgrown with crabapples and ginkgoes,
enclosed by largish iron gratings—frilly,
to say the least. From there one can spot
crumbling gargoyles that line the main building's
façade, and the arched terraces that stratify its flank.
I remembered you posing by Felisburto's "Phalanx"

at Little Five Points, that fantastic statue
of creatures eating other creatures, so modern,
and we remarked we'd never seen *decoupage*
so daring, in concrete, and on such a scale as that.
I fumbled through my pack to find the camera,
picked it out and began snapping shot upon shot.
In that hat, few women could match you.

In that skirt you looked like some spurned heiress
heading out into the night to prove she's still got it.
In pale lipstick you smacked of Greta Garbo
or Lily Dean, or a Mackelwayne sister. I waited
for you for seven years—I can barely believe it—and
you never came. And I retired to Russia, and the rest
(as they say) is hail blown across a hotel terrace.

beard beard

You loved me once
but now you don't,
because I shaved
off my goatee

and left only
a strange mustache.
I miss your love
but wonder what

it was based on—
a full Van Dyke?
A hidden chin?
You loved me for

the wrong reason.
But there's still hope.
I saved my beard.
I know, I'm weird—

I swept it up
in a Ziploc
in case you ever
want it back.

So let me know,
it's in my desk.
I'll trade it for
your love, no less.

efficiency versus thought

We looked abroad for an answer.
We zoomed in on "if the orange leaves are smitten."
We focused on *orange*.

We looked abroad to another world,
in which "porpoises shimmer in the continental glare."
And we concluded that there

was nothing in *orange* and nothing in the other image.
There were no hidden meanings locked in *smitten* or
shimmer, and nothing unseen in the creatures.

So with the help of friends we changed trajectory,
and not only that, we changed velocity.
We asked Katrina if she knew,

and then Daniel Kane, and we went to the beach
and found McManus and asked him.
"...if frost hides the leaves
and the pump's concerned handle
won't lift," he said

and then trailed off. Something about Florida.
Something about the earth's weird spinning
and a bonfire's flares,

the veil of sand, a monument
of ashes there.

asking al gore about the muse

I had my hands in the pockets
of my jeans while I spoke to Al Gore
about the muse. He had no
real advice to offer, saying all
his efforts had been foiled, too,
and his arms were folded
tightly across his chest.

I kicked the curb—we were waiting
for the same bus—and he asked
if I'd heard the phrase
"kicking against the pricks";
this phrase comes from horseracing
he explained. I said no, it's biblical.
He said well at least it doesn't
come from kicking actual penises,
because that's what he always thought,
that it was a feminist phrase.

Our bus pulled up, and in a cloud
of diesel fumes he clarified
that he is, of course, a feminist,
then ascended into the bus—
cast a glance over his shoulder as if
to say, aren't you coming, darling?
But I had stalled—the muse—the muse!

nice feet

People said, "Hey. Cute face." They said,
"Hey man, you have a pretty face."
And, "That's a really beautiful face
you have on the front of your head.

I bet you hear that all the time, though."
Fact is, I did. I also heard, "Hey guy.
That's a great big hairy red beard
you have on the lower part of the front

of your head, and your nose like a bird
poised on top of a bush, and your two gray
eyes—I don't even know what to say,"
shouted from the window of a passing cab

from time to time when I was young.
At the clubs I heard, "What a face.
Could I lick the whole thing, like a plate?
Would it be okay if I hugged your head?"

Now that I'm older it happens less
and the tone is often moribund:
"Friend, you have a good face there.
Would you like to be my friend?"

They inspect the shape of my head
in silence now—keep to themselves
how they feel. They say, "Nice feet,"
but I can tell that they're just being nice.

three things

1.
Nothing is as funny
as a summer day,
but three things
are more temperate.
One. A glass
of tap water.
Two. Your mood
after we watch
"Friends."
And three.

2.
Three things
keep me from
emailing you.
I count bad
breath and
receding hairline
as one thing,
by the way.

3.
In all the universe
there are only three things.
This is the secret
of the universe,
or as the French call it,
le secret de l'univers.

unction

Send a cruiser! There's been a crime.
Our neighborhood looks the same

as it has for twenty years, but in its
deep heart's core something's wrong.

You can hear it in the birds, who sing
their songs a bit off-rhythm, now;

see it in flowers that flame up around
each friendly driveway and walk,

they're growing crookedly, and plaid;
detect it if you stop and put the flat

of your hand on the ground, a wobble,
a curse — a stolen recipe in someone's

box? "I took it," says Norma, two
doors down. "I'm the one to stone."

We did and retrieved it from her purse,
a bit dog-eared and cinnamony, now.

So hang back, coppers; we're okay
(though Norma has seen better days).

you are you

If you are you—and you *know* you are—
then please, respect someone else's right
to be someone else. We're not all you.
Some of us are us. Well, some are proud
to be us, and some are, as they say, just us.
As in, doorbell rings, who is it, it's just us.
There's no real cause for alarm when
some of us show up at the door.
But when *you* show up, coked up, crazy,
and end up passed out on the floor
with your cell phone playing a melody
just inches from your unclasped hand,
we (the rest of us) find that we can only
observe from positions we carefully staked
out during what turned into a 14-hr party.
Some of us are asleep—some, half-awake.

lone wolf

Goodnight, moon. Or rather, goodbye.
I'm tired of the tricks you've played on me.
I'd rather go through night after night
unilluminated and just a bit forlorn,

a lone motorcyclist heading for home,
than wander among your sharp shadows,
sit on your white boulders, look down
into the silver river, any longer.

in verity

Salutations from St. Louis. The rain
has rained its white voice all day
while certain words have turned red
in my mind, certain phrases — "ants
in the cupboard," say, and "heresy."

Even so, honey retains its biting tang
and watered-down daylight pours
into a bay window in the drawing room.
So like a farmer I write and write,
casting down seed upon seed, resting

only while the dot matrix printer sings.
The song effects a drowsiness in me,
so I descend into the patterns and objects
of letters: "Dear Adrian, we miss you;
come soon; the aphids are blooming,

though the violets have roses. Honeycup,
I love you like a soft-bodied insect, I
love you in the smell of sluggy grass,
with the distance of a swing set. There is
a rotten hammer underneath the deck,

and on the wicker table a bright glass." We
nap beneath the blue spring sun, turtle-like,
while words play musical chairs in our heads;
through the screen I see a copper basket
full of limes and pears, apples and candies.

the portrait of robert preston

In the portrait of Robert Preston
the dog in his lap seems asleep,
as does a woman on a loveseat
in the background, as do trees
visible through a bay window,
presumably Preston's own window,
as does all the other foliage there,
and it leaves one to wonder:

Why is Robert Preston awake
and, in fact, bolt upright?
This is not Robert Preston
the famous military lawyer
or the Robert Preston
who stole an Army helicopter
and landed it on the White House lawn
but the real Robert Preston,

Massachusetts born, son
of a garment maker, graduate
of Abraham Lincoln High School,
almost twenty years deceased.
Why does he sit so straight up
showing the whites of his eyes
in a portrait in which
everything else drowses?

train to mehlville

I have been sponsored by a local society
to sever these melons with this black mallet.

Or pulverize them, more like, and prepare
their squooshed innards for the pies

some of the ladies are baking. But the sky
is filling with green clouds like ink

in a glass of water, and a few dark drops
have fallen and are beading up along the tops

of violets here, by an old wooden shed.
I know my wife is home busily on the phone

with her sister in Oklahoma. If it's nearly
night that means my daughter is just walking out

of her cello lesson at the old college, out
onto the darkening quad where her carpool waits.

And I am supposed to crack these cantaloupes
with all my strength for an hour? Heaven

and earth could be colliding and I would have
to cherish this humble chore as if it were

a kiss with my new bride. On that day she wait-
ed beautifully on the platform, and I was late.

tilling charles reznikoff's back yard

Tilling Charles Reznikoff's back yard
brought up a dozen lions and several patches
of wildebeest hearts.

The home itself sat lively in endless shadow,
its picture windows gazing half-wittedly
in five directions.

Inside, a phone sang triumphantly,
the sole technological hormone driving
countless blushing shutters.

But my errand had to do with grass,
so I sat and thought alone in endless shadow,
speaking to myself

On the bed of wild violet that formed a border
between Charles Reznikoff's back yard
and my own,

Making no sound. Making no sound.
Making no sound. As I stood to look around,
verbs fell everywhere.

His awkward roof repelled them blankly,
staring wakefully over the wild, half-witted yard
that formed its bed.

Downfall morphed into downpour, and of a sudden
cartoony animals emerged from thickets,
surrounding that home,

and I must have looked like a startled duck,
trees above my head whipping madly,
a car pulling up.

Such a schedule had been in my mind,
such a tedious map, that I could not even hear
the writer at work.

things that i have only one of

I have two kinds of things, she says.
I have things that I am into
and things that I have only one of.

That there is more than one thing
that I have only one of is, of
course, the irony of ownership;

the real question, though, is
where do the circles overlap?
What are the things that I am into

that I have only one of? she says,
and looks momentarily tired.
Perhaps, she muses; perhaps

there is a third kind of thing.
For I also have many things
made of leather. See? she says,

gesturing to a large collection
of leather objects. I am also into
ornithography, she remarks. Now,

does that count as a thing that I
have only one of? For I do not
have more than one ornithography.

the slick ruts

I lay prone throughout Cubafest.
Flies buzzed melodiously in and out of my
transparent head.
I lay on a shirt-covered couch.
I lay among foil and comic book pages,
appliances humming in other rooms.

Soon Layla showed up in a tricked-out car,
bade me accompany her to the fire
anthem celebration two miles
this side of Phelpsville.

I tried, I nodded. I whispered through
the clamor, *Enough, later, quiet, quite
a party, sanguine lamps...*
but it was thick and rubbery there.

The heat-soaked hexes from Mexico
rowed north in boats. The white
Texan vixens came sailing in too, on brooms.
The place was full of hicks in tuxes.

Brad, that's enough. Play it somewhere else.

smocks

"Bella et her smock, wat had paint onnit,"
grumbled Ferocio. He had been
omitting cadavers all night

Trial by Ferocio, epoxy nightmare (feminism)

galactic orbiting robot force

Just give us your name
your age and something
really funny about you

My name is Irving Berlin
I'm 118 years young
and I'm part Arabian

racing horse and I like
Count Chocula and I'm
angry about the way politics

grinds its utter Wendy
right into dead stars
as though no one cared

about anything other than
their next nonsequential
narrative compromise

Hi my name is Caine Mutiny
and I'm not an age
but my funny thing is

that no one can find me
inside my own certificate
also I like tricking

mules into boring holes
in miniature walls
with microscopic drills

a box of it

i.

Let me enjoy
this strafed cutlet,
O history buff,
because it's tender
if damaged
by your so-called
war.

Wait on the glider,
Mr. Potato Head,
and learn how to operate
your digital camera.

I am sorry
to have called you
by your maiden name!
I keep forgetting
about the woman
in our well.

O buff-of-nine-tails,
the bleary gladiolas
bend delicately at the whiff
of you. O you—
sandwich-eating
bimbo.

Well enough, gathering
point, mastodons
denying heterodoxy
until the moon
comes up, lithe scythe
of white, blanched
among the branches
of the root
beer tree.

Thou of forked beard, worn
coverlets obvious
to none but Venus, the looker-
into of apes' hearts
like ours
shaped intentionally
as raisins:

What do you want!
Sign me a sign!

As I eat.

ii.

A tremendous
amount of work
went into this event.

His pool irons
bubbled, literally,
to think of your advent.
The distance
seemed like agitprop
announcing itself
as a new god
buried in unwashed
scrubs, toxic
handlebars and milquetoast
banshees also in
pile.

Assembled pylons
resisted description!
They knew of you, too,
and if not for them,
even children

would have cheered!
Toc toc toc of the raisin
clock, its big plastic
boner above the mantel,
as if time slept
at your beck
while the other dogs
chanced to sleep
on your back porch,
figuratively speaking.

Figure in the air.
Witches in helmets
eating all the parades
of airborne insects
that happened to pass
within range of
their tongues.

iii.

Death by car,
Mr. Head, and I, Ms. Body,
glumly debating
whether to return to Dubuque
by train or by glyph
or by spotted strophe

or to wait as a nymph
for your package
or you
or for your words
of promise to reglue
the stallions back into stallions
and the sheds into fewer
but larger sheds.

I claimed your barns
even before you glommed
onto my fortune
by designating land

as parquet, slicking it with tears
of goats as you'd done
back home.

By gum, I'm alone again.

iv.

You'd told me to wither
in the clamp, and that'd be
exactly what I'd have done
if not for splotches
of resin that caught
      my tail
against the grinder,
keeping me sinful
but bubbly with youth.
My eyes opened to
reveal pies,

O recordist of other women's fates,
clarinetist by the cloudy lake
at the bottom of which
she might live
yet

if you'll permit me to wax.
I like to wax this way
when I've lost your tracks.
You went off the trail

and into the moonlight's
buggy pail of milk.
The house
rested pedantically
like a three-breasted
manatee.

Cheap shottz.

v.

Yet you finally arrived
with your trix, a multiheaded
Bubba Sparxxx whose jaundice
never shows because his
retelling speaxxx distractedly
of the women at Key Biscayne.

If I, settling into night
with but this chop,
fail to refuse you, love's anchor,
with one hot gesture in the gloom,
where am I but inside
another man's room?
Awaiting yuletide's
champion
to clear my name? The game
has taken hopscotch
to its last theoretical breeding ground,
albeit its own stamping
    ground:

watch the glinting
forxxx descend
like the apple cheeked storxxx
that brought up us/
  bailed
us out

and finally grooved you
in my grout

even if manacled
by ballad rhythm
and shorn
by flimsy spout.

slam dunque

I parked my Slam Dunque by the curb.
I walked up to the waitress of the dunes
and asked for a twilight chill,

and she cortisone shotte, ye olde Candie Shoppe.

the postman

"Hello," announced the in-ground sprinkler.
"I want to be turned on that I may water
the grass and bushes now!" it shouted,
startling a serpent sleeping nearby. The serpent
uncoiled and quietly slid through the grass
toward the postman's leg and bit it.
The sprinkler simultaneously exploded water
from its shimmering, metallic top. "I'm
spraying!" it declared gleefully. The postman,
now prostrate on the ground, spluttered
and spat in the artificial rain. "A snake,"
he explained, "has bitten me on the leg.
Whether I shall walk or run again is not my worry.
Whether I shall live to see another day is.
I am a man with a wife and two children!
And is this the fate a man like me deserves?
I have been faithful and true, discharged
my duties in a wholesome and diligent
way all of my life. And is this the fate
that I deserve?" As he spoke the sky
opened up and real rain mingled with false.
Ah, it was a sight to behold: a man lying
on the ground, a redundant sprinkler,
a pile of melons carefully painted to look
like a suburban ranch house, and a snake—
yes, a common garter snake—snoozing
contentedly under a butterfly bush, its fragrant
four-parted, bell-shaped, purple flowers
with orange centers—its flower spikes erect,
ranging from four to ten inches in length—
a snake, a safe snake, really just a joke snake.

a pile of trees, and an actuary

There once was a pile of trees.
Nearby, an actuary was dancing
and cursing his Cheverly,
which had sprung a leak
in its rotary sparkler syndicate
and was rusted all to hell.

The pile of trees said, "Sirrah!
Ecoutez. Underneath me is
a police force. Under the police
force, but not near the wet ground,
near the dry ground, not near
the wet ground, is a pan of cakes.

"TAKE the pan of cakes and
speak the name of your wife
into it. Close your eyes and
pick up the first cake that
comes to hand, bite into it,
and you will find a key.

"The key is to my pickup truck.
Walk 1.5 miles that way
and get my truck and drive
it back here. I need a ride
to the Michael Bolton show.
I have a VIP pass and I need a ride."

i met katharine hepburn
for cocktails last night

I met Katharine Hepburn for cocktails last night
I was on crutches but she didn't seem to mind
she had developed a bad case of the shaky head
and wasn't about to judge me just because
my left calf was swollen like a dolphin
and I in turn certainly wasn't about to judge her
just because she looked like she was saying no
all the time for instance when the bartender
asked if she wanted another and then left
thinking she had angrily shaken her head at him
and she looked at me and shook her head
as if to say bartenders these days then she
said she loved my leg it reminded her of Caruso
I said in what way she said it's smooth
I told her that was a stretch and she said
not as far fetched as what you're thinking about
and I said so what am I thinking about
and she said every guy thinks it you know
and she said you want to sleep with me
and I said I was NOT thinking about that
and she shook her head apparently in disgust
but added that she liked me but it was her
time of month and could she take a rain check
and I asked her if she was serious about that
after all she was very famous and beautiful
and she shook her head—all things considered
we had a nice discussion and in parting
she told me I should rest my messed up leg
and gave me a friendly sideways hug and
I kissed her cheek one time when it came my way

looking at ducks

It is good to look at ducks.
I never said that I do everything right.
I said I do some things right
and that the rest is a wash.

Meanwhile, I do look at ducks
and never regret my choices.
Okay, I regret one of my choices,
but it had nothing to do with you,

and it was totally understandable.
I also regret something I said
about stars and ducks and about the sky
looking down upon the earth

the way a monster looks at a child
from within a closet, eyes glinting.
The eyes, I thought, were stars,
and in that scenario we were the ducks.

But we are not like ducks, and perhaps
in a different sense we don't even *like* them,
but I would still contend that it's okay
to look at them, even if a bit fondly,

the way a man looks at a child
who's scared in bed—consolingly.
For while we are not like them now,
we must realize that we once were,

so please excuse me while I look at ducks.

"as cole becomes less of an anomaly and the large car slows"

Every human body faces the same basic challenge:
What to do with all those sensory impulses.

I spent one summer returning them to their sources
uninterpreted. That begat a chemical depression

that lasted well into the autumn, however,
which in turn begat a small ferret named Jonathan.

One odd thing about Jonathan was that he had glasses,
(I am using the past tense because he is no longer with us)

and also he collected hockey togs and key chains.
You don't expect a ferret in a cage to peer

at you through bifocals, but this one would, and he'd
intone, "Aaron? Listen here. Accept the impulses.

They won't hurt you ultimately. Pretend they're
passing through you. 'Enjoy them while ye may,'

as the other large-scale ferrets like yourself say"
(Jonathan remained confused on this point until

the fateful day of his appointment, his departure date,
when he was Zambonied into the ice, and all I

could think was, "Hey Jon. Accept the impulses!"
Of course, inside my heart, I chastised myself for that.)

Today the so-called sun sends pieces or waves of light
into my retinal cortex and deep into my brain, for it is

summer again, and the spice bushes reek of cumin,
and all the boats in the harbor are swaying in unison.

pans

I'm still depressed
about identity politics,

and now I can't
find the cookie sheet.

I was going to bake
Pacific Islander-American

cookies as a surprise
for when Rudy gets

home but now I'll
have to use the biscuit

pan—some surprise.
The buds on the

hibiscus bush say,
as they open, "Identity

politics. Identity—"
So I close the window.

shifters

As Stephanie continues to blow peanuts through her nose,
the audience knows all too well what she is up to.

One of our children has a tree stump for a head.
It's weird, but she also has little clumps of hair, so
that's reassuring.

One sonic night in the back of our sonic house, two sonic
birds got to cawing, and before you could call the sonic night
watchman, there was a sonic burger restaurant collapsing
in a nearby strip mall: no coincidence.
Asterisk that in your diary.

Here is a pirate boy at the door. "Here, pirate boy. Here's a
penny for your pocket. Go back to your frigate now.
Go back to your barge. It's a glorious day."

Four little myths tried to explain each other. Two got talking.
"If you're so endemic, why split anthropological hairs?
I would think such excavations would come natural
to you!" said one. The other: "Yeah, and you're a pimp."

I began walking to the basket suitcase. Unfortunately
the basket suitcase was eighteen miles south. To complicate
this odyssey, I was heading east. Now calculate:
two young girls learn to jump rope in a pickle patch.
If I have neither silver nor Bundt cake in my pouch
packed for journeying, how long till coyotes
emerge from the thickets? Think!

Here is a second tale of the basket suitcase.
  In it, I am a woman trying to speak of envy
    in a Houston airport, in public, but I am naked.
      Apparently my basket suitcase has been stolen.
        I whip a cell phone out of my purse and call 911.

Jasmine and juniper, jonquil and june bugs,
  japing jesters, jelly jars, and jukeboxes jingling,
    jobless rates rising, jaundiced elderly voters,
      jerks joking jollily, janes jumping johns.

Glug! goes the periwinkle. Glub! go the radishes.
  Glug-glug! goes the fishy, and Glurp! go the tomatoes.
    Glurk! goes the paring knife, all swaddled in wax paper.
      Glug! goes my dad while he watches soap operas.

Lilly the glutton has attempted to befriend me.
  Lilly has no belly button: that's what's unique about her.

I would like for once to for once to for once.
  I would like for once to for once.
    I would like to for once, you know!
      For once in my life!

Abby at the dude ranch was looking like a snowflake.
  Her sweater smelt of pine cones, she held a plastic rake.
    The dude ranch full of snowflakes drifted high upon a fence.
      Now can anybody tell me where my Abby wence?

Each of my feet has a nose and a mouth.
  That's what's weird about each of my feet.

A simple man rose from his simple couch to drink a simple gin
in his simple domestic environment, amongst books
full of denotatory words, beneath simple shingles
plunked and spattered by elegant raindrops
on a thoroughly complex and chaotic Saturday evening.

Bozo has no heart. That's why he shoots children with his machine gun.
I have come to hate Bozo. Not for what he does, specifically,
but for the sheer fact he has no heart.

Beethoven hates children. Beethoven eats them like cookies.
Beethoven is my name for the dragon that lives behind my house.

Do not express yourself mildly: do it wildly.
Neither eat chocolate cake nor sleep among bed sheets.
For we are entering a period of sporadic vomiting
when bed sheets and slicks of dog shit in the grass
are indistinguishable. Winding bed sheet,
winding bed sheet, go back to your shelf!
Help me to forgive myself!

Druggist: "That's a taper." Pizza man: "That's a Bundt cake."
Disc jockey: "That's a small moon." Old man: "That's no small moon."
Disc jockey: "Then it's a taper." Old man: "It's not a taper."
Druggist: "Eat my shorts." Pizza man: "Eat my pizza."
Old man: "Eat my cloak." Disk jockey: "That's a space station."

"Wow," says Stephanie, nostrils flaring.
"I want to dine with you now."

tim and the giant horse

Part of me wants to eat the horse.
Part of me wants to pet it.
Another part of me wants to kick Tim with my knife-shoe
and then to defenestrate him.

I can't stop worrying about Tim on top of the horse.
Part of me wants to photograph it,
but another part of me wants to forget it.
I guess the problem is that I love that old horse.

Wait, "defenestrate" actually is a word,
it means "to throw someone or something out of a window."
Picture something you want to defenestrate:
Now imagine me doing that to Tim

after I've knife-kicked him.
But I sit here just pulling on my little beard
wondering, in part, where giant horses come from.
Also, maybe where I can get a *book* about horses.

Theoretically, let's say giant horses come from region X.
Let's say it takes Y hours to get there at Z speed.
But there's a possibility that you shouldn't be going Z speed.
Perhaps the limit is something lower.

Then again, perhaps giant horses come from *nowhere*.
I'm kidding, of course, but listen to this:
according to the web, certain women *do* come from nowhere.
Among them is a real-life queen named Jessica, who rules X

with an iron scepter. But two facts complicate the tale:
(1) The scepter is a pair of scissors. (2) Jessica is a man.

henry the eighth

I.

I sat with my head sort of hanging—in the tiled atrium.
I sat in the tiled atrium—with my head sort of hanging.
In the tiled atrium I sat with my head hanging—sort of.

Sort of hanging my head I sat in the tiled atrium.
I sat sort of hanging my head in the tiled atrium.

Buffalo cheese, buffalo cheese. Buffalo cheese.

I sat with my head sort of hanging—in the tiled atrium.

II.

III.

IV.

She sat in the wide gondola, its colorful hood
playing gaily in the breeze.

In the wide gondola she sat in the breeze playing
gaily its colorful hood.

Henry James.

V.

VI.

Monster cheese, monster cheese, we sculpt our monster cheese.

VII.

As we went, however, in her gondola,
gliding there under the sociable hood
with the bright Venetian picture framed on either side

   by the movable window,

I could see that she was amused by my infatuation.

VIII.

Henry the Eighth.

the waste land

If I had been T. S. Eliot, I wouldn't have written "The Waste Land."
As myself, however, I do plan to write it, but not with a typewriter,
and I will never turn it over to Ezra Pound's manic red pen.
In fact, I will not even publish "The Waste Land." Instead,
I'll whisper it to white doves that constantly appear at my window
wearing bib overalls and green mesh trucker caps, the ones
chewing bits of hay and sighing that they've had a scant harvest.
Then I will write "The Canterbury Tales" for vocal ensemble,
eat part of it and set fire to the rest on my kitchen table.
If I had been Geoffrey Chaucer, I would have worn Chuck Taylors
and ripped up jeans and winked broadly at my shyest students.
I would not have written "The Canterbury Tales" or "Troilus
and Criseyde," "House of Fame" or even "Parliament of Fowles";
I would have been busy drinking my daily gallon of wine
or dispensing it to the dames of Kent with the expectation
that they would get really drunk and try to pants me. Pantsed,
I would hop on them or at least play hopscotch with them
well into the wee hours as the Kentish stars winked down at us.
If I had been Shakespeare, though, I would have written "Hamlet."
That was a good idea, all things considered. Kudos to Shakespeare.

my best wand

Of all the magic wands
I've bought over the years,
only the steel one
with the sharp tip
really works—you point it
into someone and say
ABRACADABRA
and the person magically
becomes wounded.

thirty illegal moves in the cloud-shape game

Potatoes

Waves

Ghosts

A Rorschach blot

Fuzz

Clouds

A dragon head

Chèvre

A puddle

Cloth

A swab

Crumpled up paper

A blob

Trees

Jelly

Scallops

Fungi

Hair

Milk

A piñata

Chamois

Sheep

Feta

A fist

Algae

Alsace-Lorraine

Quiche

Stew

Bubbles

Pudding

five beginnings of jokes

1. Why did the elk, deer, chipmunks, coyote, sea stars, orca whale, sea lions, newt, weasel, and many different kinds of birds cross the street?

2. Elk, deer, chipmunks, coyote, sea stars, an orca whale, sea lions, a newt, a weasel, and many different kinds of birds walked into a bar.

3. How many elk, deer, chipmunks, coyote, sea stars, orca whale, sea lions, newts, weasels, and many different kinds of birds does it take to change a light bulb?

4. Elk, deer, chipmunks, coyote, sea stars, an orca whale, sea lions, a newt, a weasel, and many different kinds of birds were entering heaven, and St. Peter stopped them to ask a question.

5. What do you call elk, deer, chipmunks, coyote, sea stars, an orca whale, sea lions, a newt, a weasel, and many different kinds of birds at a party?

vittles

Considering how little new there is to say about varmints
perhaps one can write something new about vittles,
or if the mood of the room in which one is writing
is cast perfectly for such an occasion one might even
venture to write something new about vittles that also
discusses or touches upon the interests of varmints,
for varmints are known to prefer certain vittles over others
and to reject some vittles entirely, such as anything leafy.

Leafy edibles might not even be properly defined as vittles,
in which case one inevitably turns one's attention to parsnips.
Rumor has it that there is a certain kind of varmint that,
while unilaterally rejecting leafy edibles, will in fact partake
of a parsnip if the mood in the room is cast perfectly
for such an occasion, or indeed if the white china is so white
as to remind that varmint of the moon and set him to baying;
he might even partake of bay leaves if that is the case.

Bay leaves, however, and in fact parsnips themselves,
have traditionally been associated with critters,
what with the diet of critters being almost entirely leafy
and not at all thought of as vittles. It is almost comical
to imagine a critter munching on vittles. Let's say,
however, that you're stumped for ideas for your writing;
in this case, you might try picturing in your mind
a critter eating vittles—or a varmint eating leafy edibles.

Such fancy performs the function of a mental crowbar,
that is to say, it can if you allow it to perform that function:
you will suddenly remember three or four really sucky
moments of your childhood that you had suppressed,
and they will arrive in your mind with their own lexicons
and their own contextualizing power that is so overpowering
as to recontextualize even your recent thinking about vittles
and all the new things you had hoped to write about them.

mr. fibitz

I no longer say that my beer
has "head"; I say it has a foamy
top. I say there is a goodly froth
in the uppermost portion,
that it seems almost whipped.

No, I don't say that my beer
seems "whipped" or that it has
"head," even as I never ask
if people are "coming."
"I am having a big party—

are you coming?" seems
horribly confusing to me.
I ask them if they "plan
to attend," and when they
get there and begin to tap

my keg, I warn them that
they'll get a lot of "froth"
or "foam" if they're not careful.
And when they ask how
I'm doing, I never say,

anymore, that I feel "gay."
I just don't put it that way.
I never use the phrase,
"standing erect," either.
I say, "standing straight up."

I also never refer to my
donkey as an "ass," nor do I say
that I'm planning to "ride
some ass" if what I mean
is that I'm going for a ride

on Mr. Fibitz. Nor do I ever
use the word "mount"
to indicate getting on Mr. Fibitz.
I don't even say "getting on"
Mr. Fibitz anymore. It's confusing

for the listener, and the listener
is whom I care about. However,
sitting erect on Mr. Fibitz I do feel gay,
happy enough to ride him for hours—
it's just no longer what I say.

worms

Cyclists, as a rule, think bikers are cheating,
because they have engines. Pedestrians, in turn,
think cyclists are cheating; they use wheels.
People in wheelchairs think pedestrians
have a leg up, for obvious reasons,
but pedestrians think the same thing
about people in wheelchairs; they use wheels.
What makes people in wheelchairs unique
is that they also think cyclists and bikers
are cheating. Their disdain is uniform.
The wheelchairists' hypocrisy lies,
however, in their use of automobiles.
Everyone uses automobiles except worms.
Worms think they're better than everyone.
Worms think they're more authentic than everyone.
This is why people say worms are self-righteous.
To worms' credit, however, they aren't hypocritical,
except the ones that glide down the sidewalk
on hundreds of tiny legs, blithely ignoring
their wilted, sun-blackened comrades.
Those worms are called millipedes.
Those worms are really bad apples.

the one about the ectoplasm and the osteoblast

Some ectoplasm sits next to an osteoblast
at a bar. The ectoplasm asks the osteoblast,
"Why do you form bones?" And the osteoblast
responds, "Why are you the outer relatively
rigid granule-free layer of the cytoplasm usually
held to be a gel reversibly convertible to a sol?"
And the ectoplasm is like, "Wow, that is such
an awkward question." And so the osteoblast
goes, "Seriously, why are you? I form bones
for the same reason." The bartender, an osteoclast,
asks them what they want to drink. The ectoplasm
asks him what he recommends that's on draft,
and he says the Dead Guy Ale, it's a fresh keg.
They both break into fits of laughter. "Oh my gosh!"
says the osteoblast, "Dead Guy is a German-style
Maibock that's deep honey in color with a malty
aroma, rich hearty flavor and a well balanced finish.
Now does that sound like the kind of beer we drink?"

skee ball

It's true that I am experienced in the ways of freeform thought. However, others are equally, if not more, experienced than I. In fact, although I practice stream of consciousness in a professional way (if my way can be considered "professional"), and often enjoy observing the way other people's minds move about unhindered by reason, I'm better at doing other things, such as skee ball. Skee ball, to me, is paradigmatic. One rolls something toward an oddly confusing goal, the thing leaps unpredictably, and satisfies the 'demands' of the 'machine' to a greater or lesser degree. For some reason, my balls always hit 50 in the center or 100 in one of the upper corners. I am what's known in the world of skee ball as a 50/100 roller. Hence, I take all the tickets; I get all the teddy bears. I am the skee ball king, if you will.

a sentence about boomerangs

This morning my face, after I
tried to rearrange it by putting
the nose up here, one lip here,
the other there, etc., snapped back
into its original formation
as if fated to be that way forever,
and in the same way my schedule,
after I repeatedly tried to make time
for you by changing an appointment
here, not going to a show there,
kept returning to its original
ladderlike formation, and I wonder
if these curiously similar experiences
have something to do with the fact
that you're only an imaginary friend,
Mr. Puddlewump, or if they have
to do with the fact that yesterday all
the boomerangs I'd thrown
during the various stages of my life
returned within minutes of each other,
hitting me on the back of the head
in sequence, like dancers
that can't wait to get offstage
on a drizzly night when the audience
is tiny and the manager appears
to be drunk backstage, or not.

signal versus noise

For Norbert Wiener
a signal was something
that ought to be filtered
from noise, but for God,
at least in this life,
the signals merge with
the noise, and although
maybe that's just God's
way, it's possible God
is more like Gwen Stefani
in that he expects us
to hear, over the din
of the hip hop club
of this world, him shouting
"Holla back, girl!"
and wants us to holla
back somehow, through
prayer, or maybe just
lives of self-sacrifice.

alberto vo5

The thing I like best
about Alberto VO5
Extra Body Shampoo
is not that it contains
nutrients, nor even
that it contains shine-
enhancing nutrients,
but the graceful way
it contains them—
which is the same way
you carry bitter regret,
my love, invisibly,
allowing it to work
its way naturally
through my hair.

glowing pear

Because I am sad about the books
with tiny words along their spines

that no one ever reads because
they are too hard and not very interesting,

I am going to build myself a fort
of photographs of things I can't afford

and Post-It notes of words I know
but am not able to accurately define

and glossy pages from *Elle* and *Oui*
and also bark, sticks, berries, and leaves,

and sleep in it for fourteen days
and nights and spend that time in prayer,

thinking of all the fantastic lines
of poetry I know, remembering the nooks

I've read them in, and I'll bring a flashlight
to click on and off when I get bored,

to shine in my mouth and blow up my cheeks
and turn my face into a glowing pear.

to dream only of bunnies

To dream only of bunnies
is a kind of poverty.
To dream of red flashing lights,
and that only, is also sad.

To dream of flashing red
bunnies, however; to sleep,
and by a sleep to say
we dream of red and green

rabbits flashing, among cars,
and a friend we haven't seen
in quite a while standing
naked in their midst;

to sleep: perchance to die
in this our lonely shadow,
is basically to wake up
in a most alert way,

suddenly, and on a Sunday
afternoon, at the futon's
edge, one hand on the floor,
and to know, at last,

that one's existence
has meaning; has, not only
meaning, but importance;
has, in short, a dream

toward which to point its
prow as toward the rising sun
that, white on the horizon,
fills the water with its flashes.

regret

"I can't bear to look at you,"
she said as she ate
a banana she had
named Stephen.

about the author

DICK LEMMON

Aaron Belz (www.belz.net) is author of a previous collection, *The Bird Hoverer*. His poetry and criticism have appeared in such publications as *Boston Review*, *Christian History*, *Fence*, and the *St. Louis Post-Dispatch*. A former resident of St. Louis, where he founded and curated the Observable Poetry reading series, Belz is now an English professor at Providence Christian College in Ontario, California.